STEVEN SNAPE

EGYPTIAN TEMPLES

SHIRE EGYPTOLOGY

Cover photograph
The Khonsu Temple at Karnak, built by Ramesses III.
(Photograph: S. Thomas.)

British Library Cataloguing in Publication Data.
Snape, S. R. (Steven R.)
Egyptian Temples. - (Shire Egyptology; no. 24)
1. Temples - Egypt
I. Title
726.1'0932
ISBN 0 7478 0327 7

Published by
SHIRE PUBLICATIONS LTD
Cromwell House, Church Street, Princes Risborough,
Buckinghamshire HP27 9AA, UK.

Series Editor: Barbara Adams

ISBN 0 7478 0327 7.

First published 1996.

Printed in Great Britain by
CIT Printing Services, Press Buildings,
Merlins Bridge, Haverfordwest, Pembrokeshire SA61 1XF.

Contents

Acknowledgements

I am particularly grateful to Susanna Thomas, for photographic illustrations acknowledged in the captions, and to Joyce Tyldesley.

This book is dedicated to the memory of Professor A. F. Shore as a small repayment of the enormous debt I owe him.

The outline chronology is based on that of Dr William J. Murnane and acknowledgement is made to him and to Penguin Books for its use here.

Figures not otherwise acknowledged are by the author.

List of illustrations

Chronology

Based on W. J. Murnane, *The Penguin Guide to Ancient Egypt*, 1983.

Predynastic Period	before 3050 BC		
Archaic Period	3050-2686 BC		
		3050-2890	Dynasty
		2890-2686	Dynasty II
Old Kingdom	2686-2181 BC		
		2686-2613	Dynasty III
		2668-2649	*Djoser*
		2613-2498	Dynasty IV
		2558-2532	*Khaefre*
		2498-2345	Dynasty V
		2498-2491	*Userkaf*
		2453-2422	*Niuserre*
		2345-2181	Dynasty VI
		2332-2283	*Pepi I*
		2278-2184	*Pepi II*
First Intermediate Period	2181-2040 BC		
		2181-2160	Dynasties VII-VIII
		2160-2040	Dynasties IX-X
		2133-2060	Dynasty XI (1)
Middle Kingdom	2040-1782 BC		
		2060-1991	Dynasty XI (2)
		2060-2010	*Nebhepetre/ Montuhotep*
		1991-1782	Dynasty XII
		1991-1962	*Amenemhat I*
		1962-1928	*Sesostris I*
		1929-1895	*Amenemhat II*
		1878-1841	*Sesostris III*
		1841-1797	*Amenemhat III*
		1797-1786	*Amenemhat IV*
Second Intermediate Period	1782-1570 BC		
		1782-1650	Dynasties XIII-XIV
		1663-1555	Dynasties XV-XVI
		1663-1570	Dynasty XVII
New Kingdom	1570-1070 BC		
		1570-1293	Dynasty XVIII

		1551-1524	*Amenophis I*
		1524-1518	*Tuthmosis I*
		1504-1450	*Tuthmosis III*
		1498-1483	*Hatshepsut*
		1386-1349	*Amenophis III*
		1350-1334	*Amenophis IV (Akhenaten)*
		1334-1325	*Tutankhamun*
		1321-1293	*Horemheb*
		1293-1185	Dynasty XIX
		1291-1278	*Seti I*
		1278-1212	*Ramesses II*
		1199-1193	*Seti II*
		1185-1070	Dynasty XX
		1182-1151	*Ramesses III*
Third Intermediate Period	1070-664 BC		
		1070-945	Dynasty XXI
		945-712	Dynasty XXII
		924-889	*Osorkon II*
		874-859	*Osorkon III*
		828-712	Dynasty XXIII
		724-713	Dynasty XXIV
		713-664	Dynasty XXV
Late Period	664-332 BC		
		664-525	Dynasty XXVI
		525-404	Dynasty XXVII
		404-399	Dynasty XXVIII
		399-380	Dynasty XXIX
		380-343	Dynasty XXX
		380-362	*Nectanebo I*
		360-342	*Nectanebo II*
Graeco-Roman Period	332 BC-AD 394		
		332-30	Ptolemaic Dynasty
		332-323	Alexander the Great
		323-305	*Philip Arrhidaeus*
		285-247	*Ptolemy II*
		247-222	*Ptolemy III*
		180-145	*Ptolemy VI*
		51-30	*Cleopatra VII*
		30BC-AD 394	Roman Emperors

1

Introduction

The Egyptian temple, with its massive pylon entrance and pillared halls, is one of the most instantly recognisable buildings of the ancient world. It suggests strange gods and forms of worship which are alien to us today. It represents the attempts of the Egyptians to come to terms with divine power in the cosmos, attempts we can perhaps sympathise with through our own religious beliefs and the places of worship in which we express them.

Modern conceptions of religious architecture are based around the idea of special buildings or designated spaces within which ritual activities connecting the human with the divine are performed. These activities may include communal worship and, perhaps, the idea of levels of 'sacredness' within the building. The building itself may be relatively plain and indistinguishable from other assembly halls, like some nonconformist meeting houses; it may have specialised architectural features particular to the functioning of the cult, for example the mihrab and minaret in the mosque; it may be the repository of particular relics, for instance the Torah in a synagogue; and it may carry paintings and statuary which can emphasise or add to the general ambience of worship or specific aspects of belief connected with it, as do statues of saints in medieval cathedrals. The form of the Egyptian temple is influenced by many of these concerns; it is a space for specialised cult activities, but its architectural form and decoration are also vital in conveying aspects of accepted belief to the spectator. This accepted belief can include what we might term political propaganda, ideas about how the cosmos is ordered and specific myths connected with that particular temple. Form and decoration link each individual temple with others in terms of a general background of belief, while having its own particular concerns. No two temples are identical, yet none is completely unique.

There are several different types of Egyptian temple, the two most important being the cult temple and the mortuary temple. The cult temple is the easiest for us to understand for it is the place where a particular god or gods resided and where cultic activities took place, which we might term 'worship'. The mortuary temple, in contrast, was the royal version of the mortuary chapels attached to private tombs, and its most basic purpose was to provide offerings for the use of the dead king and ensure his beneficial survival in the afterlife.

Temples, and other places of worship, are built only when the religious

1. The god Sobek, from the temple at Kom Ombo.

ideas of a community become concrete enough to encompass an organised relationship between humans and the divine. In Egypt this relationship can be seen as reconciling a particular paradox. On one hand the gods and goddesses of Egypt could embody the elements and great forces of nature, such as the sun, the sky, the earth or the river Nile, or they could be deities with control over fundamental aspects of human experience, like Osiris, god of the dead. On the other hand these deities were also regarded as behaving in a very human way and with the same needs. They are often found in family groups and they looked to their devotees for the same range of domestic service as a potentate, and in definite fixed places, the house, the palace or the temple.

The Egyptians used a variety of terms to apply to different types of temple, but without absolute consistency. The most common expression for the temple itself was *hwt-nṯr*, 'the god's mansion', while the word *pr*, the simple Egyptian word for 'house', or *pr-nṯr*, 'the god's house', could also be used for the temple structure itself, the enclosure within which it was set, or the estates and lands with which it was endowed. These terms demonstrate that the temple was seen as the house of the god in a very real sense; on one level the god *literally* lived within the temple – he or she was physically resident in the cult statue housed in the sanctuary, the very heart of the temple. This statue, made of precious materials, would be the focus of the daily temple ritual of washing, clothing and feeding the god performed by the temple priests, the *hmw-nṯr* or 'god's servants', just as would have been done for the king or great lord by his servants. The Instruction of Ani, a New Kingdom text, is explicit about what a god would require from his worshipper: 'Song, dance and incense are his foods. Receiving prostrations is his wealth.'

The role of the temple as the physical home of the god is reflected in the appearance of a temple of the New Kingdom; the open courtyard, pillared hall and hidden sanctuary might be said broadly to coincide with the parts of an ordinary Egyptian house, with the semi-public space for entertaining visitors and the more private areas at the rear of the house, such as the bedroom. One function of the temple was to house the image of the god and to hide it from the uninitiated, that is everyone apart from high-ranking temple staff and the king, but by the New Kingdom it also provided a kind of divine theatre for the revelation of the god on particular stage-managed occasions when the public was allowed to approach the divinity more closely. So a temple needed to provide, in the words of Barry Kemp, both a 'realm of the hidden image' and a 'realm of the revealed image'. Ideas about the revelation of the image became more important in the New Kingdom, and the architecture of the temple altered to take account of this. Changes in emphasis between the different functions of the temple, added to royal interest in the divine, were the major reasons for alterations in the form of Egyptian temples from the Predynastic to the Graeco-Roman Period, more than three thousand years of both continuity and change.

Servants of the god

Egyptian religion, as practised in temples, was basically concerned with the performance of cult ceremonies, usually three times a day at dawn, midday and sunset, with varying degrees of elaboration. During these ceremonies the divine image was tended, food offerings were presented and incense was burnt before the god's statue and the statue itself was washed and dressed. The vessels and other equipment used for these ceremonies were usually kept in special storerooms within the temple, sometimes referred to as 'treasuries'. The people who carried out these ceremonies were the priests, but their role was much more limited than might be expected: they had no pastoral duties, nor were they interested in the spiritual concerns of the community as a whole. Their religion was not directed by divine revelation expressed in holy books and moral codes and they were little concerned with theology.

2. (Above) Ramesses II, offering to the barque of the god Osiris at his cenotaph temple at Abydos. (Photograph: S. Thomas.)

3. (Left) A priest, wearing his panther skin of office, from the 'white chapel' of Sesostris I at Karnak.

Theirs was a religion of liturgy and the performance of ritual and recitation.

In most provincial temples, particularly before the New Kingdom, these priests would have been largely autonomous; during the New Kingdom it was generally accepted that all priests were acting on behalf of the king, who was technically the High Priest of every god in Egypt, because the monarch could not be physically present to perform the daily rituals in every temple in the land.

The basic requirement of a priest was physical purity; the most common rank of priest below the *hm-nṯr* seems to have been the *wab* priest, whose title, meaning 'pure', reflects the state of physical cleanliness required of those performing rites within the temple. This cleanliness involved purification through washing and the rigorous shaving of both head and body. Although the priests were not celibate, sexual contact rendered them unclean until purified and sexual activity within the temple itself was an act of sacrilege.

There were more specialised roles within the priesthood, such as that of lector priest, distinguished by a sash worn across the chest, whose duties involved reading the appropriate texts during the ceremonies. At all periods priestly titles were commonly held by high-ranking men, presumably as an aspect of their civic duties. High-ranking women were also involved in religion: in the Old Kingdom many well-to-do women were priestesses of the goddess Hathor, while women of similar rank in New Kingdom Thebes often bore the title 'Chantress of [the god] Amun'.

The staff of an individual temple could vary greatly in size according to locality and period. Most small, local cult temples would be primarily staffed by so-called 'hour priests', local part-timers working on a rotating shift system who usually served for one month in four and who were organised into four priestly shifts called *phyle*. The Middle Kingdom temple of the god Anubis at Kahun was probably typical for a provincial temple of the period in having a permanent staff of six priests and forty-four part-timers organised into four rotating shifts. The permanent staff of temple administrators and performers of the most specialised rituals was probably quite small, so that the staff of an average cult temple in the New Kingdom might amount to between ten and twenty-five individuals. Most provincial part-time priests lived away from the temple, but the professional priests often had housing provided within or close to the temple precincts.

The more important national cults, begun as cults to local town or regional gods, became significant national institutions based at major cities. As the town itself became more important so its patron deity or deities rose to national prominence and royal patronage of a god and its temple was a guarantee that the cult would become more important. In this way the more significant deities achieved their pre-eminent status

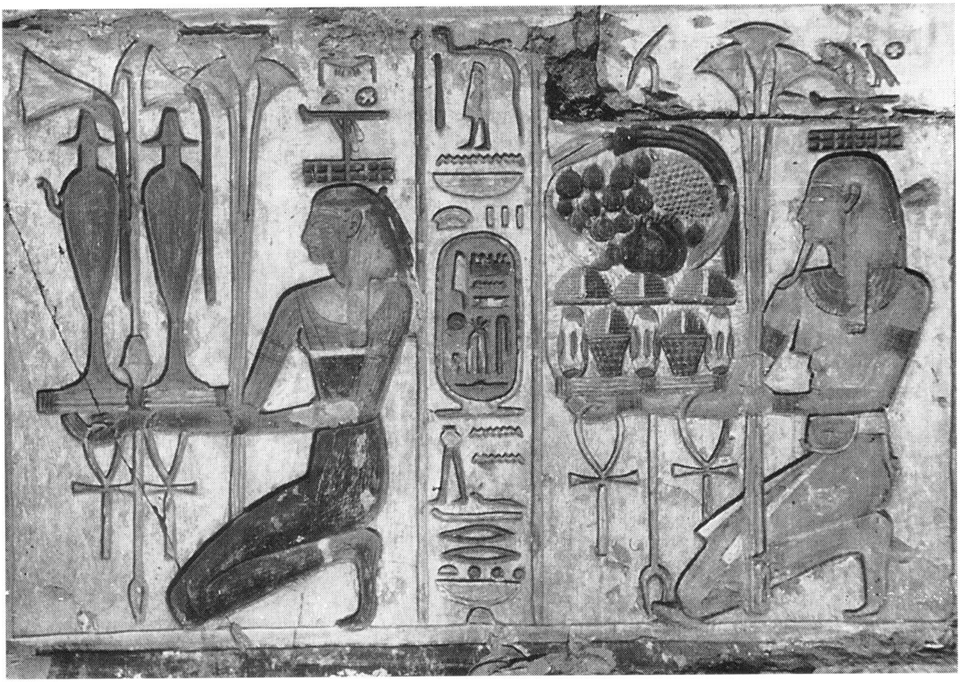

4. The wealth of Egypt, symbolised by deities personifying the regions of Egypt bearing agricultural products, is offered by Ramesses II in his cenotaph temple at Abydos.

among the ranks of Egyptian gods and goddesses, such as Re at Heliopolis, Ptah at Memphis and Amun at Thebes. The highest ranks of their priesthoods were largely hereditary and politically important and often bore individual titles, like the High Priest of Ptah at Memphis, called 'Greatest of those who supervise the Craftsmen', and the High Priest of Re at Heliopolis, who was the 'Greatest of Seers'. These temple institutions needed substantial numbers of ancillary staff to produce the offerings presented in the temple and to maintain and extend the fabric of the building. For such temples, a staffing level of between one and two hundred might not have been unusual; in the New Kingdom the estate of the god Amun, based at Karnak, employed more than 81,000 individuals.

Temple economy

Substantial resources were required for paying the wages of all these priests and other temple officials, providing the offerings themselves and maintaining and extending the temple. Most of our evidence for temple funding comes from the New Kingdom, when it is clear that major temple foundations were endowed by the king with the economic resources required to make them self-sufficient. This endowment was

5. Temple magazine at Zawiyet Umm el-Rakham, containing Egyptian and foreign storage vessels.

chiefly in the form of land – the most certain wealth generator in the ancient world – the produce of which would form both the offerings to the gods and, by a process known as the 'Reversion of Offerings', the rations which formed the wages of all the god's servants, from the highest priest to the lowliest labourer working on the temple building. Any surplus could then be distributed as largesse or traded. The Great Harris Papyrus recorded donations of roughly 300,000 hectares of land by Ramesses III to temples. The bulk of this (240,000 hectares) went to the estate of Amun at Thebes, with most being used for the benefit of the king's own mortuary temple at Medinet Habu on the West Bank. This land would be used to produce the valuable basic commodities: grain for bread, beer, cakes and animal feed; fruit and vegetables; and flax for linen. The Medinet Habu temple, for instance, had a regular daily income of over 8000 litres of grain, enough to feed approximately six hundred families, plus meat and other comestibles. Temples could also acquire luxury goods from abroad and mineral wealth through endowments of mines and quarries, while donations of prisoners of war provided a useful pool of labour. To house this wealth, temples of the New Kingdom were equipped with substantial mud-brick storerooms. In this way temples became important economic and political institutions within the Egyptian state, and the priesthood which managed them can be viewed as one of the more significant branches of the Egyptian civil service.

2

Archaic Period and Old Kingdom temples

The Djoser complex and primitive temples

The building which allows us to trace the origins of monumental architecture in Egypt most clearly is the Step Pyramid complex built for King Netjerykhet Djoser of the early Third Dynasty. This is a landmark building in every sense: the first stone building of any size to be constructed by man, the first pyramid and ancestor of all later pyramids, and the first expression that has survived to us of a monumental tradition which embodies much earlier architectural archetypes. To understand the significance of the Step Pyramid complex we must consider its basic constituent parts.

A limestone enclosure wall, with tall niches in the 'palace façade' decorative style, contains an area of approximately 146,000 square metres. Within this enclosure is a complex of buildings including the Step Pyramid itself, which does not directly concern us here, and a series of more intriguing structures. The mortuary temple, immediately

6. A 'dummy' shrine from the Step Pyramid complex of Djoser at Saqqara. (Photograph: S. Thomas.)

to the north of the pyramid, served as an offering place for goods and services rendered on what was intended to be an indefinite basis to the soul of the dead king. To the south-east of the pyramid is the so-called 'Jubilee Court'; this consists of a series of dummy buildings (figure 6), whose function has been widely debated. It is most likely that they are recreations in stone of structures which would originally, that is in their 'real' forms, have been made of much flimsier materials, with walls and roofs of matting and reeds supported by thin papyrus-stalk columns.

This is an architecture which encapsulates in stone the ancient forms of temples associated with the gods. It seems likely from the evidence of early illustrations on wooden and ivory tablets and sealings, and from recent excavations, that most early temples were built in mixed media. The primitive shrines, which could be portable, were hut-like or animal-shaped frames, made of wattle, daub and skins. These could be erected in enclosures of mud-brick, where larger wooden and some stone elements were no doubt also in use. Very few temples of the period before the Old Kingdom have survived, with sites such as Hierakonpolis, which has a late Predynastic desert ceremonial centre, and Elephantine, where an Early Dynastic shrine was set in the rocks of the cataract, being the exceptions in Upper Egypt. So far, no early temples have been identified in the Delta, where the damp environment is not conducive to preservation, although mud-brick architecture has

7. Hieroglyphs from the temple of Edfu representing the ancient prototype for temple architecture, the primitive shrines of the Archaic Period. (Photograph: S. Thomas.)

been discovered at Buto, one of the ancient religious centres. It may be that the dummy buildings in the Step Pyramid enclosure represent the archaic shrines of early gods; in any event, what is significant is the idea of archetypes of architecturally primitive structures evoking an idea of the ancient and eternal in the divine. This is a theme which, much later, influenced the iconographically sophisticated New Kingdom and Graeco-Roman periods, where the forms of these ancient shrines survive in the hieroglyphic script (figure 7) and in architectural details in later stone temples such as the 'torus-roll' edging to pylons, representing tightly bound bundles of reeds.

Hierakonpolis

Certainly the most enigmatic and probably the original cult temple of the Protodynastic Period is that in the city of Hierakonpolis in southern Egypt. It seems likely that the early shrines were situated east of a circular mound of clean sand enclosed by a sandstone revetment, which is in the same relationship to them as the Step Pyramid is to the Heb Sed court of Djoser. Votive offerings by early kings to the gods of this temple were buried, most famously in the 'Main Deposit', whence came commemorative mace heads and palettes of monarchs of the unification period (*c.* 3050 BC). Traces of stone structures erected by Khasekhemwy of the Second Dynasty were found south of the revetment. These were followed, probably towards the end of the Old Kingdom, by the construction of mud-brick chambers over the mound. This early temple is important because Hierakonpolis was a major regional centre for the south of Egypt during the successful annexation of the north and may have acted as a national shrine. The main deity was Horus the falcon, a god who gave kings like Narmer victories in the same way that their distant successors would benefit from the help of Amun of Karnak.

Royal mortuary temples of the Old Kingdom

For kings of the Old Kingdom there was no question that the royal pyramid complex should receive the greatest effort in terms of building work. But though the mortuary arrangements of these kings are well known through the massive pyramids forming the tomb of the king, it is important to recognise that a pyramid had other buildings attached to it which were also vital to the functioning of a complex of related structures. These were the mortuary temple, almost always sited on the eastern side of the pyramid, and the valley building, which was at the eastern end of a long causeway stretching from the mortuary temple towards the valley of the Nile and usually on the banks of a canal. The best surviving example is that belonging to the pyramid of King Khaefre at Giza (figure 8). Khaefre's valley building is the best-preserved temple of the Old Kingdom, consisting of a roughly square building of local limestone faced with huge slabs of granite, brought from the quarries at Aswan in the very south of the country. Granite was also used for the monolithic square columns and architraves of the T-shaped internal hall (figure 9). The valley building was probably used during the funeral for rites of purification, while the twenty-three statues of the king originally in the building were used for rites connected with giving the king the use of his faculties in the next life. Khaefre's mortuary temple, connected to the valley building by a causeway 400 metres long, is the first in the Old Kingdom to have the developed basic five-part plan of columned entrance halls, central open cloistered courtyard, five niches (probably for statues of the king), five storerooms, and a niche in the sanctuary to which offerings would be made for the *ka* (spirit) of the king within the pyramid.

This basic format continued to be used for mortuary temples attached to pyramids of the Old and Middle Kingdoms (figure 10), although it became more complex as mortuary temples grew in importance and pyramids declined in size.

The sun temples of Abu Gurob

Perhaps the easiest cult temples of the Old Kingdom to understand are those erected by some of the kings of the Fifth Dynasty (*c.* 2498-2345 BC) just to the north of the main pyramid site of that period at Abu Sir, part of the Memphite necropolis. Despite, or

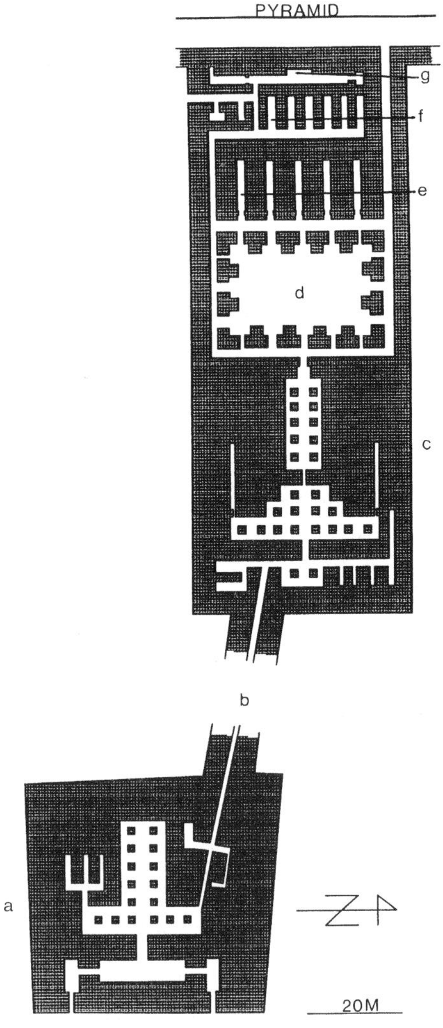

8. Plan of the mortuary temple and valley building of Khaefre at Giza: a, valley building; b, causeway; c, entrance suite; d, open court; e, statue niches; f, storerooms; g, sanctuary and offering niche.

perhaps because of, being built of stone, only one of these buildings is in a recognisable form today, that belonging to King Niuserre (figure 11), although it is known from inscriptional evidence that six sun temples originally stood here. The sun temples were designed for a type of cult which appears

9. (Right) The interior of the valley building of Khaefre at Giza.

10. (Below) The mortuary temple of Sahure at Abusir, looking eastwards over the temple, along the causeway towards the tree-filled pit marking the site of the valley building.

throughout Egyptian history, the worship of the sun god Re. Re was particularly favoured by monarchs of the Old Kingdom, and it may be that the architecture of the sun temples at Abu Gurob reflects the form of the most important temple of this period, that of Re at Heliopolis. The site of the Heliopolis temple is known from later additions to it, but the Old Kingdom structure has been almost completely destroyed. Re did not need a hidden image within a sanctuary because the sun god appears every day in the sky, but he required an appropriate place where the sun could be worshipped and a cult symbol which was a representation of the sun and its rays. The Re temple at Heliopolis contained a cult object, the round-topped *benben* stone, which seems to have been a focus for worship. In the sun temple of Niuserre the *benben* stone was replaced by a massive squat obelisk of stone masonry, standing at the rear of the main temple building, providing a focus for the cult. In front of the obelisk is a huge alabaster altar in the form of four enormous *hotep* 'offering' hieroglyphs, pointing as much to the sun itself as to the obelisk (figure 12). Fragments of decoration from the temple celebrate the beneficent influence of the sun on nature.

However, this sun-temple form is by no means original; it is approached by a causeway leading from a valley building and the obelisk is within a rectangular enclosure wall and surrounded by ancillary

11. Reconstruction of the sun temple of Niuserre at Abu Gurob. (From F. W. von Bissing, *Das Re-Heiligtum des Königs Ne-Woser-Re*, Berlin, 1905, plate 3.)

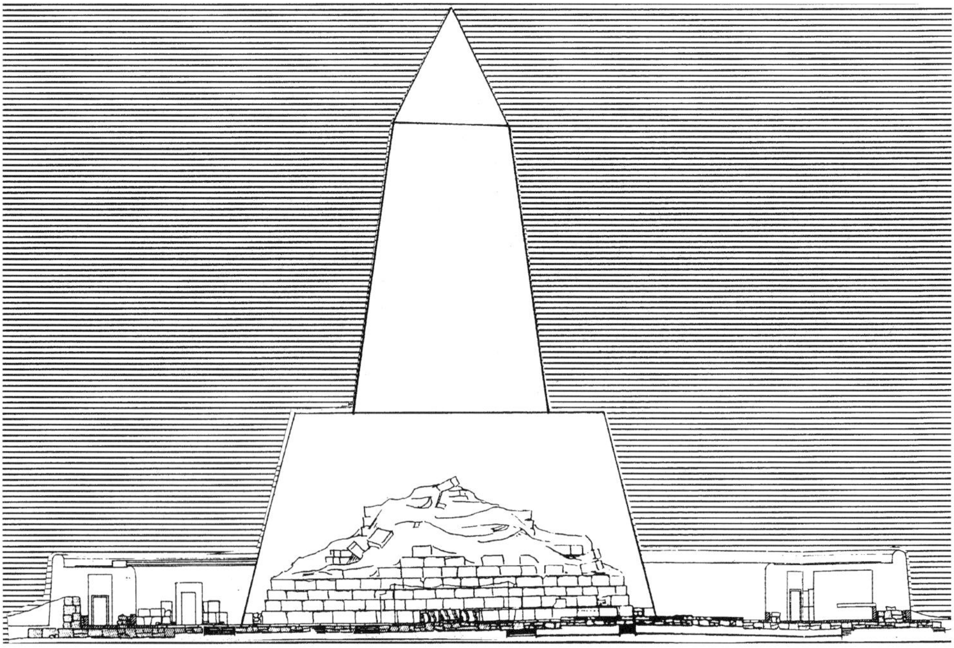

12. The great alabaster altar of the sun temple of Niuserre at Abu Gurob.

buildings. The building took as its architectural model the form of a standard pyramid complex of the Fourth to Sixth Dynasties. The architect of the sun temple of the Fifth Dynasty was using the architectural vocabulary which already existed for a royal tomb complex. The pyramid complex also, at its heart, had a form which was almost certainly derived primarily from solar imagery, the pyramid itself.

Apart from the pyramid complexes and sun temples, few temple buildings erected by Old Kingdom monarchs have survived; one exception is the small limestone temple erected for the *ka* of the Sixth Dynasty King Pepi I at Bubastis in the eastern Delta (figure 13). The mud-brick chambers at Hierakonpolis, in one of which life-size copper statues of Pepi I and his son were found, may have also been connected with this cult.

Medamud

The most peculiar, yet in some ways the most typical, cult temple of the very few which have survived from the Old Kingdom is at the site of Medamud, just to the north of Thebes. It is probably typical to the extent that, unlike Heliopolis, Abu Gurob and the mortuary temples of the pyramid complexes, it was not the subject of direct royal interest.

13. The *ka* temple of Pepi I at Bubastis.

Away from major metropolitan centres and sites of royal concern, provincial cult temples were built using mud-brick and serviced by local officials acting as priests for local deities, the 'town gods' often invoked on Egyptian stelae. Untrammelled by the constraints of an existing architectural tradition, the forms of these provincial temples were moulded round the needs of the particular cult. At least this is suggested by the temple at Medamud, which, in use probably until the end of the Old Kingdom, bizarrely consists of an irregular polygonal enclosure (figure 14), filled with trees and containing two mounds. Each mound contains a single small chamber at its centre, which is reached by a winding sand-floored passageway. These two passageways have their entrances in a courtyard, at the front of which is one (later two) pylon-like gateways. It is assumed that this odd construction served the local needs of the particular cult; unfortunately we know nothing of the deities worshipped at Medamud at this time, although later the town was an important cult centre of the falcon-headed Monthu, also worshipped in other parts of the Theban nome.

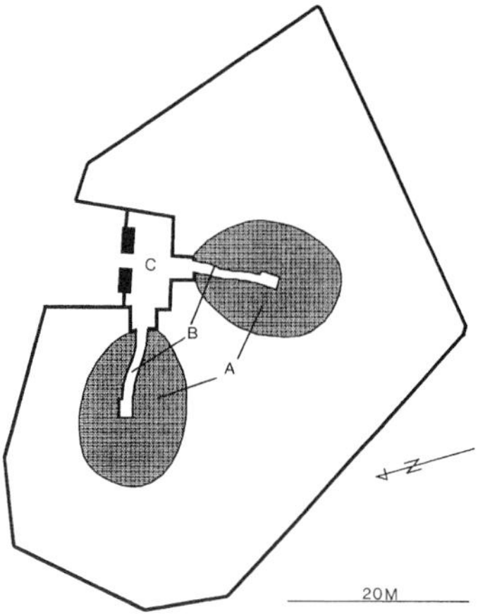

14. Plan of the Archaic and Old Kingdom temple at Medamud: A, the mounds within the temple enclosure; B, the sand-floored passageways and internal chambers; C, the courtyard with pylon gateway.

3

Middle Kingdom temples

Temple building in the Middle Kingdom is characterised by a number of important features. One is the reintroduction of the pyramid-complex form by kings of the Twelfth Dynasty, which represents a deliberate attempt by these kings to use architecture to stress continuity with the Old Kingdom. The pyramid complexes of Amenemhat I and Sesostris I at Lisht clearly look to that of Pepi II at Saqqara, which was effectively the last substantial pyramid of the Old Kingdom, as their model. However, unlike what appears to have been the case in the Old Kingdom, there seems to have been a greater royal interest in provincial temples in the Middle Kingdom, attested archaeologically by the increased use of stone, which was a virtual royal monopoly. Also, despite an increasing regularity of form seen in the comparison between the polygonal enclosure of Medamud of the Old Kingdom and the symmetry of Tod of the Middle Kingdom, the Middle Kingdom was still able to produce buildings of strikingly original character, the best example of which is one of the earliest, the combined mortuary temple and tomb of King Nebhepetre Montuhotep of the Eleventh Dynasty (figure 15). This

15. Aerial view of the mortuary temple and tomb of Nebhepetre Montuhotep at Deir el-Bahri.

16. The obelisk of Sesostris I from the temple of Re-Harakhty at Heliopolis. (Photograph: S. Thomas.)

building, set at the back of the natural 'bay' of the Theban mountain on the West Bank at Deir el-Bahri, consists of a central square-based (pyramid?) superstructure, surrounded by an elaborate colonnade, with a further colonnaded hall running to meet the cliff surrounding the entrance to the burial chamber. The terraced form of this building seems to have been the immediate inspiration for its better-known and better-preserved neighbour immediately to the north, the mortuary temple primarily built by Queen Hatshepsut in the Eighteenth Dynasty.

Sesostris I, second king of the Twelfth Dynasty, was the first Middle Kingdom monarch to initiate a large-scale building programme of temples throughout Egypt. Stone blocks from his temples have been found in over a dozen locations, from Elephantine in the south to the Delta in the north. The most striking survivals are fragments of larger-scale works at the two most important religious centres in Egypt: a solitary obelisk within the enclosure of a now disappeared temple for Re-Harakhty at Heliopolis (figure 16), and the so-called 'white chapel' (figure 17), a magnificently fashioned limestone shrine which was later dismantled and used as builders' rubble in the third pylon at Karnak.

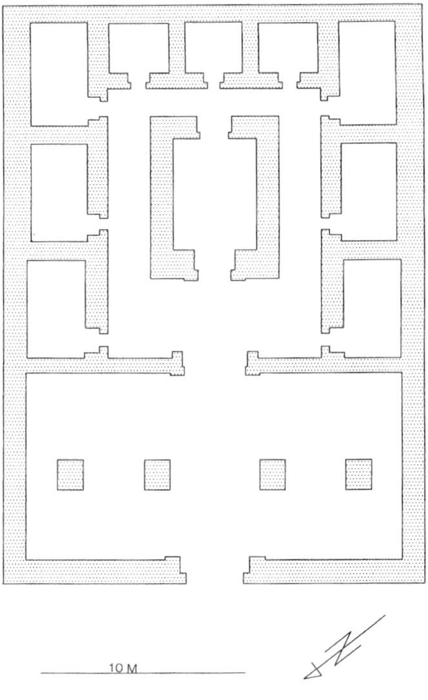

17. (Above) The 'white chapel' of Sesostris I at Karnak. (Photograph: S. Thomas.)

18. (Right) Plan of the temple at Tod.

Perhaps a more typical product of the reign is the temple at the Upper Egyptian site of Tod. This site has also produced a granite pillar bearing the cartouche of King Userkaf of the Fifth Dynasty, possibly suggesting the original existence of now lost building works in Upper Egypt by Old Kingdom monarchs. Sesostris I's temple for the god Monthu at Tod is striking in its symmetry around the central axis (figure 18). A hall containing four pillars stood before the rear part of the temple containing the sanctuary and rooms for cult equipment.

At Hermopolis Magna in Middle Egypt King Amenemhat II showed his devotion to the god Thoth by adding a limestone gateway and mud-

19. Plan of the temple at Medinet Maadi.

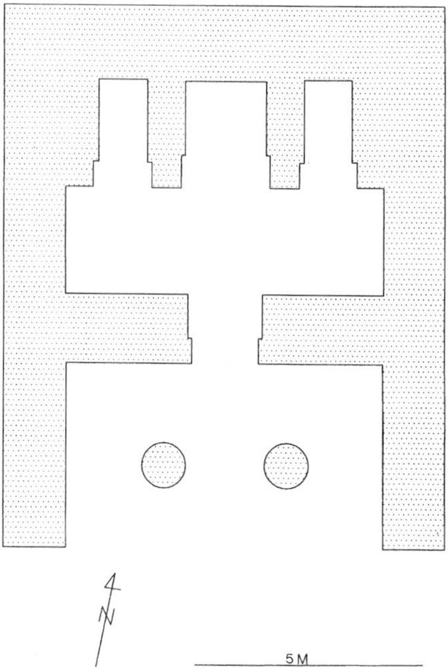

brick enclosure to the god's temple there. Kings Sesostris III and Amenemhat III continued the Twelfth Dynasty building tradition, particularly in the newly developed region of the Fayum, which seems to have especially benefited from royal patronage; the more widespread use of stone for temple building here may well be a sign of this royal favour. A good example from the Fayum is the work of Amenemhat III and Amenemhat IV at Medinet Maadi (figure 19). Although only 8.5 by 11 metres in size, the stone temple has a small shrine fronted by a courtyard with two papyrus-bundle columns with 'bud' capitals.

20. Reconstruction of the colossi of Amenemhat III at Biahmu. (After W. M. F. Petrie, *Hawara, Biahmu and Arsinoe*, London, 1889, plate lxxxiii.)

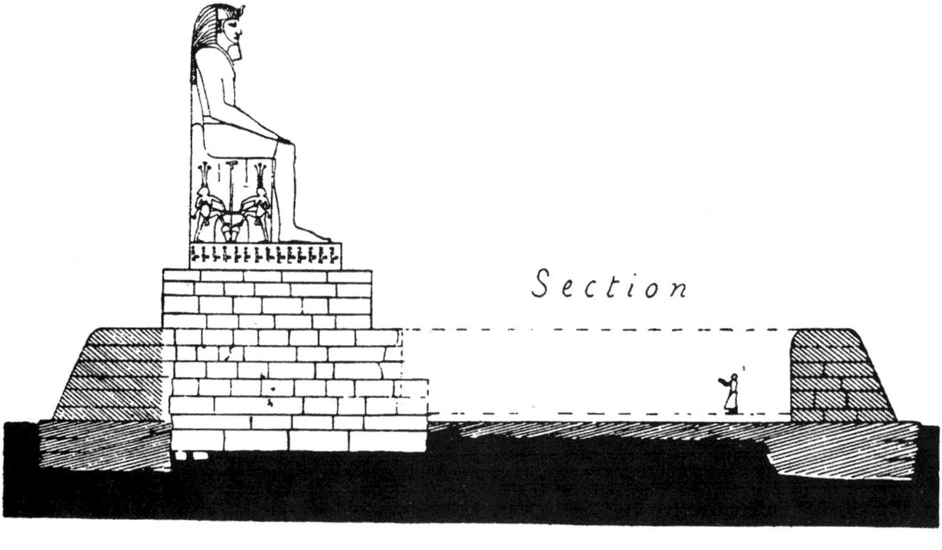

21. Plan of the Middle Kingdom temple at Ezbet Rushdi, showing two building phases in mud-brick and limestone doorways and column bases.

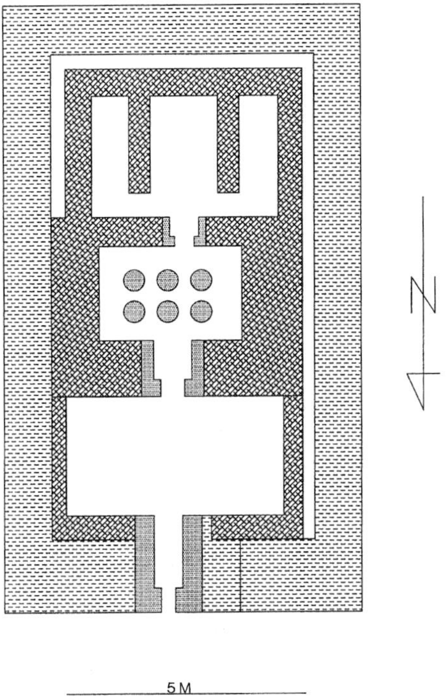

Other striking examples of similar date in the same region include the unfinished temple at Qasr es-Sagha and the two colossi of Amenemhat III at Biahmu. The latter site seems to have consisted primarily of two adjacent 34 by 39 metre precincts, each of which contained a plinth over 6 metres high on which stood quartzite seated statues of the king 11 metres tall (figure 20).

Middle Kingdom cult temples in the north are even rarer than those in southern Egypt and the Fayum. One exception is the brick-built temple possibly founded by Amenemhat I, and certainly added to by Sesostris III, at Ezbet Rushdi in the eastern Delta. This mud-brick structure, with limited stone elements in the doorways and columns, seems to foreshadow New Kingdom temples with its courtyard, columned hall and sanctuary arrangement (figure 21). The presence elsewhere of whole or fragmentary statues of kings is a fair indication that there were temples in the Delta which have now disappeared. Good examples are fragments of colossal statues of Amenemhat III at Bubastis. However, the Middle Kingdom statuary excavated at Tanis is now thought to have been transported there a millennium later.

4

New Kingdom cult temples

With the New Kingdom the Egyptian temple comes of age. The massive building programme embarked upon by kings of the early Eighteenth Dynasty was continued by their successors throughout the New Kingdom. The scale of temple building by individual kings can be regarded as an indicator of wealth and royal power during their reigns, with high points under Amenophis III and Ramesses II and low points during the decline of the late Twentieth Dynasty.

Kings of the early Eighteenth Dynasty clearly wished to be directly involved in the construction of individual temples in the regions; this represents a distinct shift from Old and Middle Kingdom practice where most royal interest was centred on a few major monuments, especially the royal pyramid complex and perhaps a limited number of important cult temples with royal connections, for example Heliopolis in the Old Kingdom and Karnak in the Middle Kingdom. The aspiration of kings to patronise temples throughout Egypt found its most concrete expression in the large-scale use of stone as the primary building material. Modest

22. Gebel es-Silsila. The horizontal cuttings of the sandstone quarries can be seen halfway up the cliff, above the rock-cut chapels of the New Kingdom.

stone temples or stone elements in basically mud-brick structures, which typified pre-New Kingdom cult temples in the regions, were now replaced by much more ambitious temples constructed almost entirely of stone, especially sandstone from the quarries at Gebel es-Silsila north of Aswan (figure 22). The process is typified by a building inscription of Tuthmosis III from Karnak which reads: 'Lo, my Majesty found this temple built of brick ... My Majesty ordered that the measuring-cord be stretched anew over this temple, it being erected in sandstone.'

The 'standard-plan' New Kingdom cult temple

A major development at Thebes was the appearance of the 'standard-plan' cult temple, a form which continued into the Graeco-Roman Period in the south, as at Edfu. The major features of this standard plan can best be seen in a simple example, the temple constructed by Ramesses III for the god Khonsu within the Amun enclosure at Karnak (figure 23 and cover illustration). Here a massive pylon gateway stands in front of an open colonnaded courtyard, at the back of which a densely columned hypostyle hall acts as a screen in front of the sanctuary which housed the divine image. These four elements (pylon, courtyard, hypostyle hall, sanctuary) are the basic parts of a standard-plan temple. However, the dominance of this architectural form in the south may not be representative of the architectural forms of temples in the Delta during the New Kingdom; the paucity of surviving evidence from the north makes such assumptions unreliable. Moreover, the standard plan was probably never thought of by the Egyptians as a firm blueprint for temple design but was merely a collection of individual architectural units which satisfactorily served their particular functions. Variations on the theme were the norm rather than the exception, especially in major temples, like Karnak, which were added to and altered by successive kings.

The extensive use of stone for the walls and columns of New Kingdom temples also made possible their decoration with carved and painted reliefs. These reliefs, which seem to cover almost every square centimetre of available wall space, provide a series of texts and illustrations which help both ancient and modern observers to interpret not only the function of individual parts of the temple but also, in a wider sense, what the building means in theological terms. This theology of the temple worked on a series of different levels. At its broadest, the temple is a recreation of the landscape of creation, the place where, at the 'first time', land arose from the waters of chaos and order (*maat*) was created from chaos. This is most clearly expressed later in temples of the Graeco-Roman Period but was also an aspect of royal involvement with New Kingdom temples. The king's main task was to maintain *maat,* and he did this by an explicit contract with the gods; they made him king by

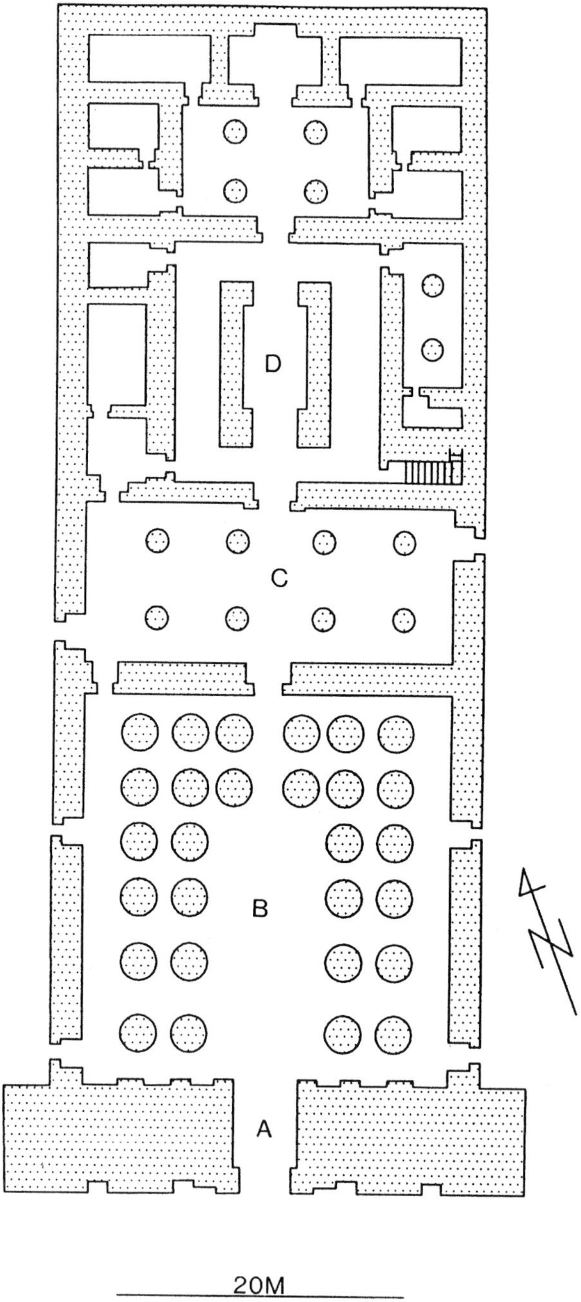

23. Plan of the temple for the god Khonsu at Thebes:
A, pylon gateway;
B, colonnaded courtyard;
C, hypostyle hall;
D, barque sanctuary.

putting him on the 'Horus Throne of the Living' and ordered the natural world for him by providing the regular inundation of the Nile. He, in return, acted in an appropriately kingly way, which included the building of temples and making sure the altars in those temples were provided with offerings for the gods. Thus the act of temple building was an essential activity in the maintenance of *maat* (figure 24). It is not surprising that the temple could also act as the place of coronation for a new king as Luxor Temple was used for the coronation of King Horemheb at the end of the Eighteenth Dynasty.

The idea of the temple as an epitome of the cosmos is clearly seen in its decoration; ceilings are covered with stars, columns take the form of papyrus and lotus (both marsh plants), while the floor level of the temple rises as the sanctuary is approached, the sanctuary being mythologically linked to the mound

24. Nectanebo I offers *maat* to the god Thoth.

where life began and, more tenuously, to the presence of mound-shaped structures in earlier cult temples such as Hierakonpolis and Medamud. It may also be that the great mud-brick enclosure walls which define the sacred precincts around temples and kept out the uninitiated often take an undulating form not for any constructional reasons but to mimic the waters of Nun, the primeval ocean, from which the temple rises as the island of first creation. Real, rather than symbolic, water is sometimes found within the temple enclosure in the form of a 'sacred lake', which could be both a 'pure' source for ritual cleansing and a place for aquatic processions of the deity. Cosmic symbolism can be detected in other aspects of temple architecture; solar concerns affect the front of the temple where the sun rises or sets between the twin towers of the pylons, which are usually oriented east-west or west-east. Thus the combination becomes a gigantic representation of the hieroglyph for the horizon, with the sun between the two hills of the pylons, and where the sun also shines along the temple axis towards the sanctuary.

The form of a standard-plan New Kingdom cult temple can also be described in terms of the physical performance of its cult. The role of daily service of the divine image as the major function of the cult at all periods has already been described; it was joined in the New Kingdom by the idea of festival. It is likely that festivals of their patron deities were held at all cult temples at particular times during the year. The royal appropriation of major regional temples meant that a whole range of different festivals were now performed in any given temple: festivals celebrating the operation of *maat* in the natural world with the arrival of the inundation, royal festivals such as jubilees, and the traditional festivals of the gods themselves. The involvement of the general population in these festivals was an important aspect of their operation, but one which was problematic, given the exclusive nature of New Kingdom cult temples. However, the main manifestation of festival was procession; the god left the temple and was, to a limited extent, seen by the multitudes both inside and outside the temple.

25. Map of Thebes, showing the major cult and mortuary temples of the New Kingdom: a, mortuary temple of Seti I at Qurna; b, mortuary temple of Hatshepsut at Deir el-Bahri; c, mortuary temple of Ramesses II ('the Ramesseum'); d, mortuary temple of Amenophis III at Kom el-Hetan; e, mortuary temple of Ramesses III at Medinet Habu; f, Karnak – enclosure of the temple of the god Amun; g, Karnak – the enclosure of the temple of the god Monthu; h, Karnak – enclosure of the temple of the goddess Mut; i, Luxor Temple; j, processional route of the 'beautiful festival of the western valley'; k, processional avenue from Karnak to Luxor.

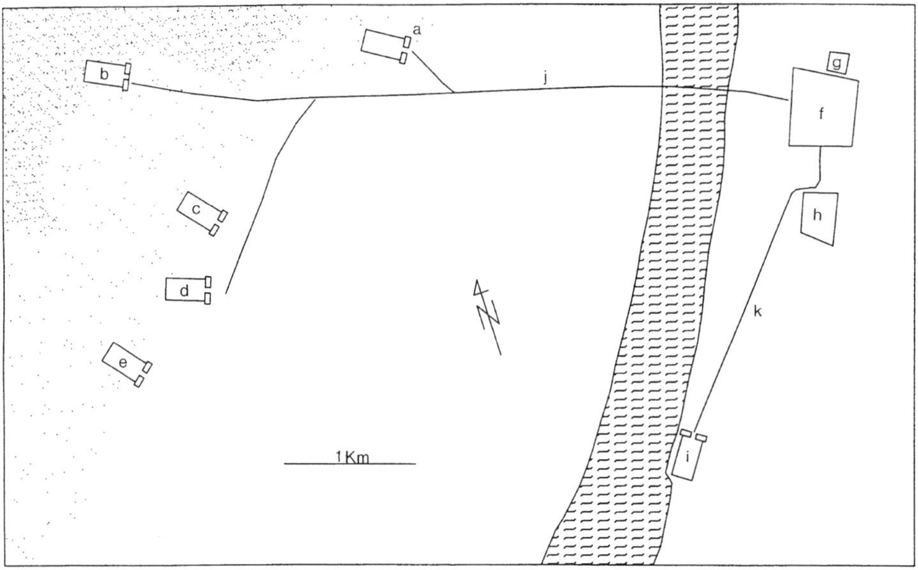

26. The pylon of Ramesses II and approach to Luxor Temple. (Photograph: S. Thomas.)

The idea of procession was a major factor in temple development at Thebes in the New Kingdom, particularly after the reign of Amenophis III, who seems to have devised a network of processions linking East and West Bank temples through festive routes (figure 25). A temple is approached by a processional way, perhaps linking it with another temple, best exemplified by the processional routes connecting Karnak with its dependent Luxor Temple over 2 km to the south, by means of sphinx-lined roadways. Those lucky enough to pass through the enclosure wall into the temple precincts would see the processional way enter the temple through its main entrance, the pylon. This consists of a relatively modestly sized gateway flanked by two massive stone towers (figure 26). The pylon was doubtless intended to be an impressive and intimidating entrance, particularly for those who could not enter, and, like the outer walls of the temple, also served as a convenient permanent billboard for royal propaganda. This might be generalised and conventional, such as the king smiting his enemies, or a more specific record like the battle of Kadesh in the temples of Ramesses II (figure 27). In either case the idea of the king acting as king in the sight of gods and men is important, contrasting with the more private aspects of the king carrying out the service of the god's cult on the walls of the inner rooms.

In front of the pylon stood examples of giant 'temple furniture', especially tall monolithic obelisks and colossal seated or standing statues of the king. These statues, particularly those of Ramesses II, were individually named; they often became the focus of cults of their own and were prayed to or invoked by ordinary people. They provided a way in which the popular cults of the great proportion of the Egyptian population could interact with 'official' religion in an 'official' setting.

27. Royal propaganda on temples; counting hands of the enemy slain on the outer wall of the cenotaph temple of Ramesses II at Abydos.

Behind the pylon was the interior of the temple. An open courtyard, surrounded on some or all sides by a colonnade (figure 28), was the semi-public area to which some people would be given limited access during particular festivals. This accessibility is suggested by the Ptolemaic name for this courtyard, 'hall of the multitude', and, in the

28. The first court of Luxor Temple built by Ramesses II and containing colossal statues, many of which were usurped by him from Amenophis III. (Photograph: S. Thomas.)

29. *Rekhyt* (lapwing) hieroglyph on a temple block, Cairo Museum.

New Kingdom, by the large *rekhyt* hieroglyphs (figure 29), representing 'ordinary people', which were sometimes inscribed in appropriate places in temple courtyards to indicate to an illiterate population where they should stand while the procession passed.

30. The great hypostyle hall at Karnak, built by Seti I and Ramesses II. (Photograph: S. Thomas.)

31. Hatshepsut offering to the god Amun, who is shown within his barque shrine, from the 'red chapel' at Karnak. (Photograph: S. Thomas.)

At the back of the courtyard was the hypostyle hall, usually broader than it was deep and filled with columns (figure 30). Its practical, rather than symbolic, function seems to have been to act as a dense screening from the semi-public courtyard for the hidden rear part of the temple. The rear chambers of the temple consisted of storerooms for cult equipment and, at the very heart of the temple, the sanctuary in which the image of the god was kept. In New Kingdom Theban temples this sanctuary would take the form of a room longer than it was wide, open at both ends, and with a plinth or stand at its centre. This form of sanctuary was designed for the 'barque shrine' (figure 31), a shrine in the form of a boat, the heavily decorated cabin of which was used to house the god's image when he or she was carried in festival processions in the barque shrine. The actual image of the god was not seen, but the barque shrine must have given spectators who thronged the processional routes the sense of the immanence of the deity. This was one of the few occasions when the public could consult the deity directly; questions put to the god were answered, probably by the priests who were carrying the barque moving

32. The temple of Amun at Karnak.

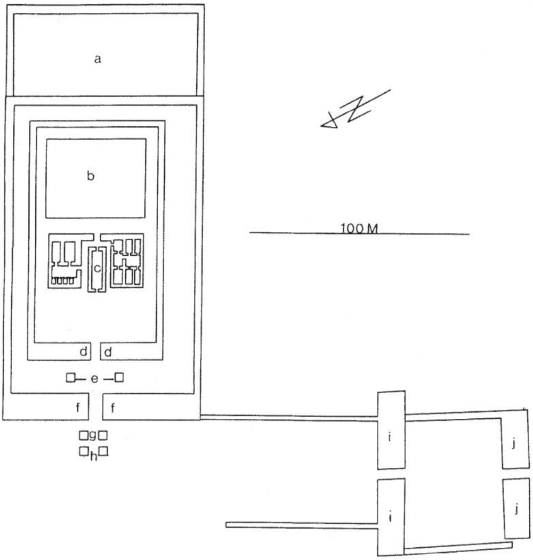

33. (Left) Plan of the temple of Amun at Karnak at the end of the reign of Tuthmosis III: a, the *akh-menu*; b, the site of the Middle Kingdom temple;
c, the 'red chapel' of Hatshepsut (if not yet demolished) and its surrounding rooms; d, pylon five; e, obelisks of Hatshepsut;
f, pylon four; g, obelisks of Tuthmosis I; h, obelisks of Tuthmosis III; i, pylon seven (Tuthmosis III); j, pylon eight (Hatshepsut).

34. (Below) Wall scene at Karnak, depicting two obelisks erected there for Amun by Tuthmosis III.

forward in assent and backwards in dissent. Resting places for the barque shrine, sometimes called barque stations or peripteral temples, somewhat similar to the 'white chapel' of Sesostris I, were located along these processional routes.

Private statues in temples

Private individuals could use statues as a 'host' in which their 'soul' could reside after death. A statue placed in the tomb was a guarantee of a physical home if the body rotted and it acted as a natural focus for offerings by relatives, friends and those employed to 'feed' the dead statue-owner. In a similar way, statues placed in temples allowed the owner to be perpetually present and able to benefit from the crumbs which fell from the divine table

35. Looking eastwards along the axis of the temple of Amun at Karnak, towards the sanctuary. The obelisk on the right belongs to Tuthmosis I, that on the left to Hatshepsut.

through the same 'reversion of offerings' which paid the priests, particularly at festival time. These statues, usually placed in the courtyard of the temple, were made of durable materials, such as granite, and their form is typified by the popular 'block statue' whose squat shape is eminently practical for a statue left outdoors and reflects the patient attitude of a worshipper awaiting the god's attention.

Karnak in the New Kingdom

Not surprisingly, it was the temple of the god Amun, patron of Egyptian kings and the newly established Egyptian empire, which benefited most obviously from the building programme of Eighteenth Dynasty kings. The Karnak complex, the detailed form of which is little known in the period before the New Kingdom but certainly included substantial buildings erected by Sesostris I, was completely restructured by kings from Amenophis I onwards. Amenophis' successor, Tuthmosis I, erected buildings at Karnak, including the pylons which are today numbered four and five, and, in front of them, a pair of obelisks nearly 22 metres tall.

Under Hatshepsut and Tuthmosis III there was an acceleration in the development of Karnak as these monarchs displayed their particular piety for the god, whom each held in special regard. Hatshepsut's claim to the throne was partly based on her being the bodily daughter of the god; Tuthmosis III claimed that he had been personally selected by the god during one of Amun's processions. Their major building works at Karnak included embellishments within the existing Tuthmosis I structure, where Hatshepsut erected two obelisks between pylons four and five and her new barque sanctuary for Amun, the 'red chapel'. Tuthmosis III built pylon six and extensions to the rear of the Amun temple, most notably the *akh-menu*, sometimes called the 'festival hall',

36. The 'tent-pole' columns of the *akh-menu* of Tuthmosis III at Karnak.

the tent-pole shaped columns of which (figure 36) may have been inspired by his military campaigning. Further additions to the Amun temple included the first major works which extended the temple to the south by creating a second axis at right angles to the main approach to the heart of the temple, pointing towards Luxor Temple, with the building of pylons seven (Tuthmosis III) and eight (Hatshepsut).

Later major contributors to the extension of the Amun temple at Karnak in the Eighteenth Dynasty included Amenophis III, who built

37. Plan of the temple of Amun at Karnak showing additions of the late Eighteenth and Nineteenth Dynasties: a, pylon three (Amenophis III); b, hypostyle hall (Seti I and Ramesses II); c, pylon two (Horemheb); d, pylon nine (Horemheb); e, pylon ten (Horemheb).

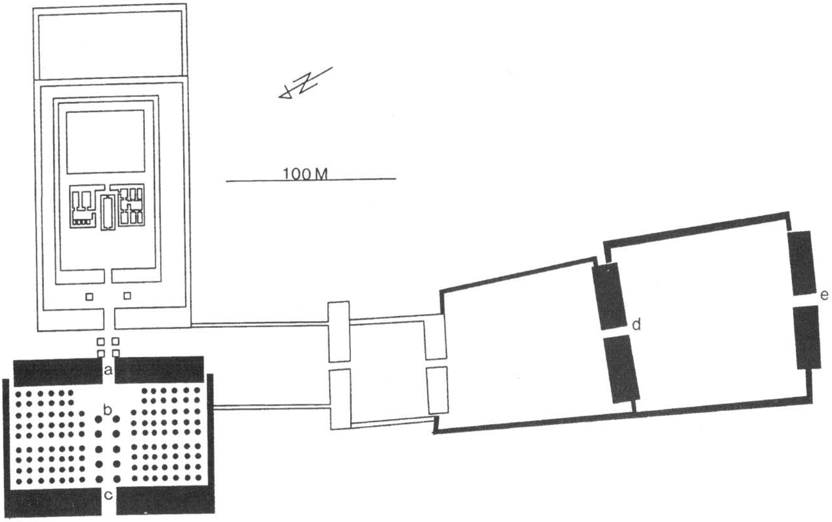

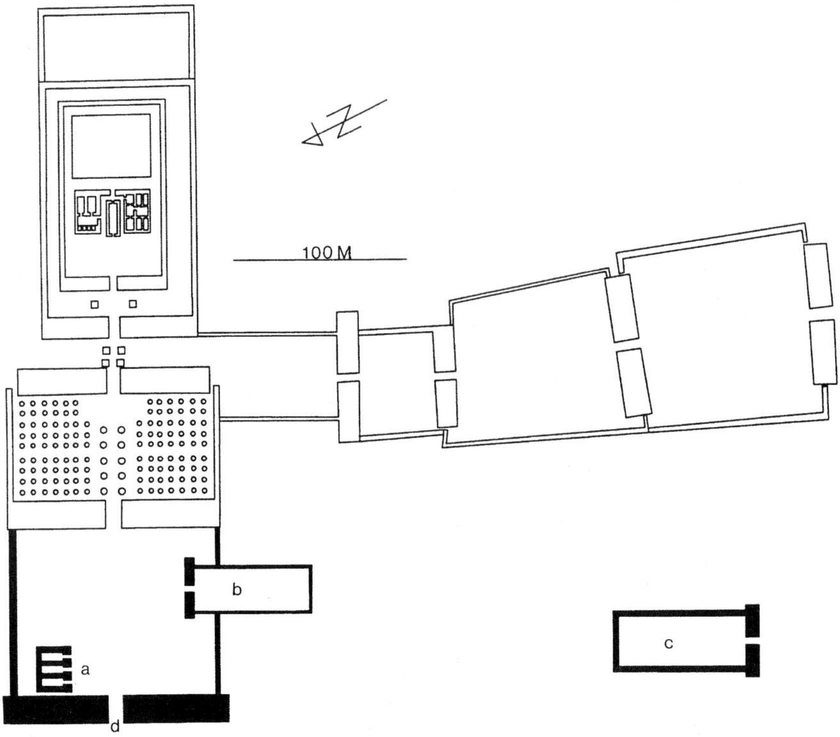

38. Plan of the temple of Amun at Karnak showing major additions after the Nineteenth Dynasty: a, triple barque shrine (Seti II); b, barque station (Ramesses III); c, Khonsu temple (Ramesses III); d, pylon one (Thirtieth Dynasty).

pylon three on the main axis and the processional streets south to the Mut complex and Luxor Temple, and Horemheb, who constructed pylon two on the main axis and pylons nine and ten on the southern axis. In the Nineteenth and Twentieth Dynasties the most significant builders at Karnak were Seti I and his son Ramesses II, who built the great hypostyle hall between pylons two and three. Seti II erected the triple barque shrine in front of pylon two and Ramesses III the barque station in front of pylon two and the Khonsu temple. Of the other major monuments to be seen today at Karnak, the first pylon was probably built in the Thirtieth Dynasty and the granite barque sanctuary, almost certainly situated on the site of Hatshepsut's 'red chapel', by Philip Arrhidaeus, half-brother and successor of Alexander the Great.

5
Mortuary temples

The most significant break in the architectural development of the royal tomb separates the Old and Middle Kingdoms from the New Kingdom and Late Period. This, in broad terms, is the abandonment of the pyramid. It happened for a number of reasons, security of the royal burial place being a significant factor. The most common term for mortuary temple is *hwt*, 'mansion'. In the New Kingdom the term 'mansion of millions of years' is often used, distinguishing it from the cult temple, 'mansion of the god'. In the mortuary temple ceremonies were carried out, theoretically for eternity, which provided offerings for the nourishment of the dead king's *ka*. Thus the royal tomb complex had two basic functions and two basic parts: the tomb itself, which was not to be disturbed and was sealed for eternity, and the mortuary temple, which was open for the activities of its staff of priests, theoretically for eternity. While the former could, in theory, easily be hidden, the latter could not. Therefore, when kings chose the Valley of the Kings as a secret royal necropolis at the beginning of the New Kingdom they had to make separate arrangements for the mortuary temple. The solution was to build the mortuary temple away from the royal tomb, thus giving no clues to its location, and in a more practically convenient situation on the edge of the desert on the West Bank at Thebes. Most of the monarchs of the New Kingdom built mortuary temples as part of their provision for the afterlife and, away from the pyramid-complex format, the New Kingdom mortuary temple developed a new architectural model based on contemporary cult temples. Unfortunately, although their tombs in the Valley of the Kings or the adjacent Western Valley remained largely undestroyed, if not undisturbed, the masonry mountains of their monumental mortuary temples proved too tempting as quarries, not least for their temple-building successors. Today few mortuary temples stand proud above ground level. The most striking example of destruction is the mortuary temple of King Amenophis III at Kom el-Hetan (see figure 25), which, although safely assumed to have been one of the most magnificent constructions anywhere in Egypt, has had all of its above-ground masonry removed, leaving two colossal quartzite seated statues of the king, which once sat before the pylon, guarding little behind them (figure 39).

Medinet Habu

The classic example of a 'standard' New Kingdom mortuary temple is Medinet Habu, a complex of buildings of varying date. At their heart

39. The 'Colossi of Memnon', seated statues of Amenophis III located in front of his now destroyed mortuary temple.

is the best-preserved mortuary temple in the Theban area, that of Ramesses III of the Twentieth Dynasty. This temple is closely based on the less well-preserved mortuary temple of Ramesses II, 1.25 km to the north-east, which is now known as the Ramesseum. The complex of buildings at Medinet Habu also includes a royal palace attached to the mortuary temple, indicating that the functioning of the temple was not limited to the period after the king's death but could be used for ceremonial during his lifetime.

The architectural configuration and decorative scheme of Medinet Habu provide ample evidence of the differences between a New Kingdom mortuary temple and an Old or Middle Kingdom version, which was part of the pyramid complex. In external appearance Medinet Habu conforms to the standard plan of Theban temples of the New Kingdom (figure 40), with an imposing enclosure wall surrounding a temple which is clearly of the pylon, courtyard and columned hall type, while its scenes and texts are similarly of a conventional, rather propagandistic type. The front half of the Medinet Habu temple consists of public views of Ramesses III on the two pylons and courtyards. These include

40. View down the central axis of Medinet Habu. (Photograph: S. Thomas.)

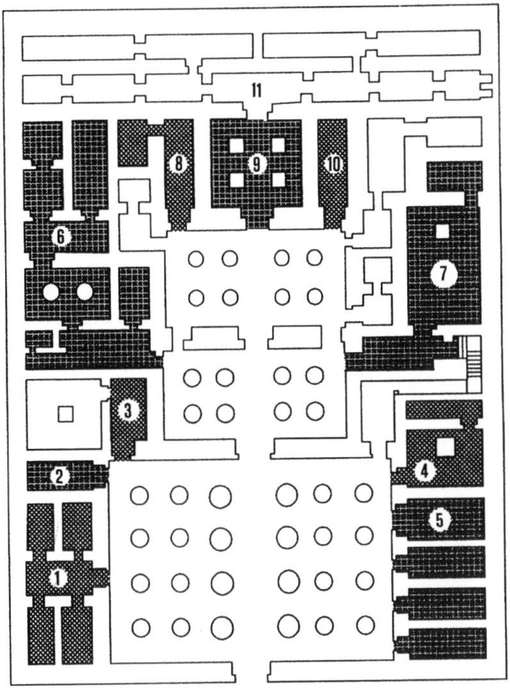

41. Plan of the rear part of the mortuary temple of Ramesses III at Medinet Habu. Rooms entered from the first hypostyle hall: 1, the 'Treasury', where Ramesses III offers rich apparel to Amun; 2, chapel for the barque of the deified Ramesses II; 3, chapel for the barque of the god Monthu; 4, 'Slaughter Court', where Ramesses III offers to the Theban triad; 5, chapels to the gods Sokar, Osiris, Ptah and the 'Living King'. Rooms entered from the second hypostyle hall: 6, 'Osiris Suite', Ramesses III with Osiris and in the 'Fields of Iaru'; 7, 'Re-Harakhty Suite', including the altar court. Rooms entered from the third hypostyle hall: 8, chapel for the barque of the goddess Mut; 9, chapel for the barque of Amun; 10, chapel for the barque of the god Khonsu. Rooms entered via the barque chapel of Amun: 11, false door, the traditional focus for offerings in a mortuary temple, with a depiction of Ramesses III being embraced by Amun. Around this false door are rooms in which the king is shown with various gods, particularly forms of Amun.

historical events, namely the Libyan War of Year 11 behind the first pylon, the Northern War of Year 8 on the second pylon and the Libyan War of Year 5 in the second court, and participation in local processions such as the Valley Festival, on the first court, and the procession of the barque of the god Ptah-Sokar, on the second court.

It is at the rear of the temple that Medinet Habu is radically different from for instance the Khonsu temple built at Karnak by the same king, for, rather than a single sanctuary or shrine arrangement for the god's image or sacred barque, the inner, most important areas of the mortuary temple deal with different concerns (figure 41). One role of New Kingdom mortuary temples was to emphasise the identification of the dead king with particular gods; the most important of these gods were Osiris and Re, who appear in the Old Kingdom royal funerary literature called the Pyramid Texts. Osiris was connected with the living king of Egypt becoming the dead king of the 'Field of Reeds'; the king became Osiris. This identification is stressed at Medinet Habu by a suite of dark rooms at the southern side of the heart of the temple. On the northern side are rooms associating the king with the god Re-Harakhty and the idea of solar rebirth; here an altar court, open to the sky, provides an appropriate architectural setting for these ideas. But if these two suites of rooms would have been readily understandable by an Egyptian of the Old Kingdom, the central suite would not; these rooms connect the king

42. Architectural statuary: a pillared figure of Ramesses III at Medinet Habu.

to Amun, the most important deity of the New Kingdom and effectively the main divine patron of the king and of the Egyptian empire, particularly here in the Theban region. But a mortuary temple was also a celebration of divine kingship, used as such during the reigning monarch's lifetime, so it is not surprising to find chapels both for Ramesses III himself and for a venerated royal ancestor, Ramesses II (sometimes called the 'contiguous temple'), to whom Ramesses III looked as a model in many aspects of his kingship.

Deir el-Bahri

Even in unusual architectural variants of the mortuary temple, the basic ideas remain consistent. This is best demonstrated in the mortuary temple of Queen Hatshepsut at Deir el-Bahri. Externally this temple is radically different in character from the classic 'pylon and courtyards'

43. The approach to the mortuary temple of Hatshepsut at Deir el-Bahri. (Photograph: S. Thomas.)

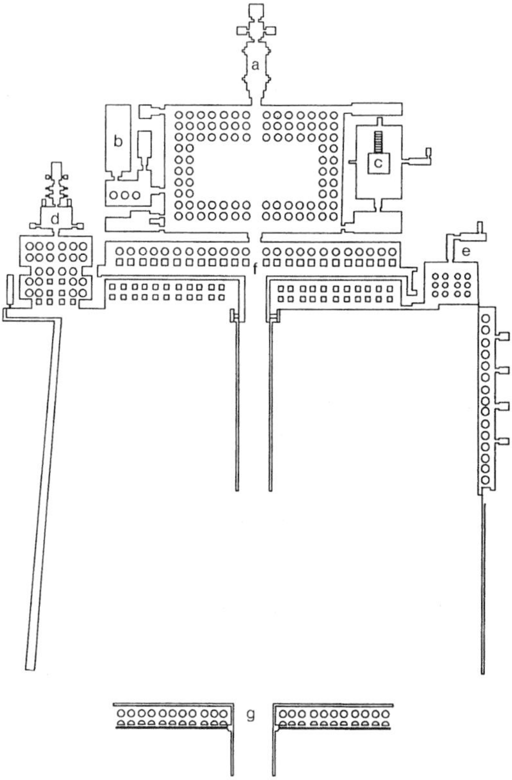

44. Plan of the mortuary temple of Hatshepsut at Deir el-Bahri: a, sanctuary; b, mortuary suite; c, altar court; d, chapel of Hathor; e, chapel of Anubis; f, upper colonnade; g, lower colonnade.

model with which we are familiar. A series of broad, colonnaded terraces retreats towards the back of a natural bay in the Theban mountain (figure 43), possibly taking their inspiration from the neighbouring, though more modest, 'terrace temple' of King Nebhepetre Montuhotep of the Eleventh Dynasty. The relief decoration in the fore parts of the temple, located on the walls behind the colonnades of the terraces, is strikingly unusual, with the transport by barge of obelisks from the granite quarries at Aswan to Amun's temple at Karnak and a record of an expedition by sea to the land of Punt, probably modern Eritrea, replacing the more conventional war scenes in a seemingly non-belligerent reign. A particular concern of Hatshepsut, a female king, was to emphasise her right to rule, and scenes depicting the divine birth and coronation of Hatshepsut make this point very forcefully. But, despite the unusual nature of the architecture and decoration of the front parts of the temple, the rear rooms of the temple are more conventional in linking the monarch both to appropriate divinities, especially Amun, and to her royal ancestors.

Cenotaph temples at Abydos

An unusual variant on the theme of the mortuary temple is the so-called 'cenotaph temple'. This type was built because the site of Abydos was so important within the system of funerary beliefs of the Egyptians. Abydos was the most notable cult centre of the god Osiris (figure 45), who was the most important of the deities connected with the afterlife. As 'Foremost of Westerners' he was the king of the underworld, the counterpart to the living king and, in the New Kingdom and later, to

45. The king worships the god Osiris at the cenotaph temple of Seti I at Abydos.

Amun-Re, king of all the gods. Abydos was considered the burial place of Osiris and, since Egyptians wished an association with the god who would have a particular importance to their survival in the next life, physical proximity to the god's place of burial was an obvious means of seeking favour. By the New Kingdom not only the king but each deceased person was 'an Osiris', and for ordinary people a substitute for burial at Abydos was to dedicate a statue within the cult temple of Osiris, or to erect small mud-brick chapels containing dedicatory stelae on the route of the procession of the god from his temple to his mythological burial place at the Umm el-Qa'ab, the actual burial place of the kings of the First Dynasty. The Egyptian term for these chapels or cenotaphs, *m'h't*, also came to be used for their royal equivalents, which were, unsurprisingly, built as full-size temples. The earliest of these Abydene royal cenotaphs seems to have been erected by King Sesostris III

46. The cenotaph temple of Seti I at Abydos.

47. Interior of the cenotaph temple of Seti I at Abydos. (Photograph: S. Thomas.)

of the Twelfth Dynasty, but the best-known and best-surviving cenotaph temples come from the early reigns of the Nineteenth Dynasty.

The cenotaph temple of Seti I (figure 46), begun by him and completed by Ramesses II, who also erected one for himself, is one of the best-preserved temples in Egypt. Its wall decoration in painted raised relief is one of the masterpieces of Egyptian art, and its form is almost unique. The basic function of the temple is to associate the dead king with the underworld gods of Abydos and with other important deities of the period; to this end the temple has, uniquely, no fewer than seven sanctuaries. Three of these are dedicated to the Abydene family of Osiris, his wife Isis and their child Horus. The remaining four were to Amun-Re and Re-Harakhty, both of whom figure largely in conventional mortuary temples; to Ptah, god of Memphis, the effective capital of Egypt at this time; and to the deified Seti himself. The cenotaph complex also includes the Osireion, a strange underground building immediately behind it, which is associated with themes of rebirth and the afterlife common to Abydos, and also to the form of a New Kingdom royal tomb at Thebes. It seems that the Abydos cenotaph of Seti I provided a solution to the problem of a king wishing to be buried at both Thebes and Abydos by providing a duplicate 'dummy' temple and tomb at Abydos which would lack only the body of the king himself.

6

Unusual New Kingdom temples

The form of conventional cult temples and mortuary temples of the New Kingdom is, as has been shown, dominated by the so-called 'standard plan'. Notable variations exist either where parts of the temple are of unusual form, for example the *akh-menu* of Tuthmosis III at Karnak, or where whole temples are presented as original and distinctive architectural works, a style best exemplified by Hatshepsut's mortuary temple at Deir el-Bahri. But in the New Kingdom other types of temple took on novel forms in non-conventional areas of religious practice and in territories peripheral to the Egyptian state.

Temples of the Amarna Period

The temple-building programme initiated by Akhenaten at Amarna after the move to the new capital in the fifth year of his reign (c. 1346 BC) is an interesting mixture of tradition and innovation in temple architecture. As always, the particular performance of the cult dictates the form of the building in which the cult ceremonies are performed. It is, therefore, natural that the form of the deity itself is particularly significant in this case. The Aten, the predominant deity during the Amarna regime, is its own image; the sun-disc in the sky, with beneficent rays reaching down to the earth, can, as it were, be worshipped from, but not contained within, the temple. The reconstruction of temple buildings at Amarna is complicated by the post-Amarna dismantling of buildings which were themselves erected quickly using smaller than usual building blocks, so-called *talatat*, many of which were reused within Ramesside temples across the river at Hermopolis Magna. However, the tombs of nobles at the northern and southern ends of the 'bay' which encloses the city of Amarna bear on their walls detailed depictions of the city and the buildings it contained, including the temple area (figure 48). These depictions, together with careful archaeological work at the site, allow some idea to be formed of the Great Aten Temple at Amarna.

The main temple was called the *Per-Aten*, 'House of Aten', an enclosure 730 by 230 metres in size which seems to have contained two distinct religious structures, although much of the interior is empty, perhaps because it was never completed. The first is the *Gempaaten*, 'The Place where the Aten is found', a long structure 210 metres long and 32 metres wide, the front part of which seems to have been called the *Per-Hai*, 'House of Rejoicing'. The *Gempaaten* is a traditional temple in the sense that it uses the basic format of pylon and courtyard.

48. The Great Aten Temple at Amarna as depicted in the tomb of Panehesy. (From N. G. Davies, *The Rock Tombs of el-Amarna II*, London, 1905, plate xviii.)

However, these courtyards, and indeed the area immediately to the south of the *Gempaaten*, seem to be unique in that they were densely packed with small stone or brick offering tables; the orientation of the cult ceremonies is not inwards, towards a sanctuary within which the deity dwells, but rather upwards towards the sun-disc itself. Comparisons with this form of temple, open to the sun, can be found in the Old Kingdom sun temples at Abu Gurob and in the altar courts of New Kingdom mortuary temples. The second major building within the *Per-Aten* temple at Amarna is now called the Sanctuary and may have originally consisted of a raised platform containing a *benben* stone. Nevertheless, it is clear that the visible presence of the sun's disc did not mean that the performance of cult ceremony was open to anyone; tomb scenes from Amarna show that this was very much the prerogative of the royal family.

Rock temples

Where steep-faced cliffs come down to the riverbank in Middle and Upper Egypt, cutting tombs from the living rock was a common practice from the late Old Kingdom onwards. The same convenient rocky outcrops were also occasionally used for small temples. These could be of two types: the *speos*, which was entirely cut from the cliff, and the

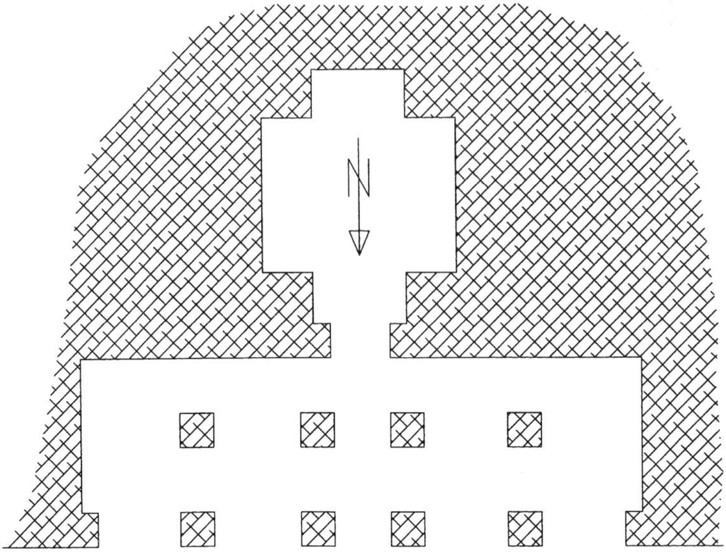

49. Plan of the small rock-cut Speos Artemidos temple of Hatshepsut and Seti I.

50. The rock temple of Ramesses II at Abu Simbel.

51. The temple within the fortress at Zawiyet Umm el-Rakham, over 300 km to the west of the Nile delta.

hemispeos, where the rear of the temple, consisting of the sanctuary and columned hall, was cut from the rock, but the front part of the temple, the open courtyard and pylon, was constructed from masonry blocks in the same way as other stone temples. One of the earliest examples of the *speos* type is the so-called Speos Artemidos, constructed by Hatshepsut, with later amendments by Seti I, for the leonine desert goddess Pakhet near the site of Beni Hassan in Middle Egypt (figure 49). But the major manifestation of rock-temple building is in the six temples of this type built by Ramesses II in Nubia; his temple at Wadi es-Sebua is an excellent example of the *hemispeos* type, while the Abu Simbel temple, fronted by four colossal statues of Ramesses himself, 21 metres high, cut from the cliff (figure 50), is both one of the most deservedly famous temples built by an Egyptian king and, perhaps, the most emphatic demonstration of the use of the temple as a means of promulgating the (semi-)divine status of that king. The Nubian temples are the most obvious manifestation of this, but temples within fortresses in less pacified border regions may partly have acted as a morale-boosting reminder of a divine military king for his beleaguered troops far from home (figure 51).

7

Late Period and Graeco-Roman temples

Temple architecture before the reign of Alexander the Great

The importance of temples of the Third Intermediate Period and Late Period (the Twenty-first to Thirty-first Dynasties) is not, unfortunately, matched by their survival and they have disappeared in a more dramatic way than those of the preceding New Kingdom and the succeeding Graeco-Roman Period. Part of the reason is their location; in the period following the New Kingdom the economic importance of the Nile Delta was equalled by its political pre-eminence. This was particularly true of the Third Intermediate Period, when several cities of the Delta were home to rival dynasties, each claiming the throne of Egypt, and in the Late Period several were the home town of the king of a unified Egypt and benefited from the patronage of their favourite sons.

The most important new temple complex of the Third Intermediate Period is that at Tanis in the north-eastern Nile Delta (figure 52). Under the Twenty-first and Twenty-second Dynasties it had pretensions to be the 'Thebes of the North' and to rival Karnak in its patronage of the god Amun. To embellish the temple, monuments were imported from other parts of the north of Egypt, including the temples of Ramesses II at Pi-Ramesses, sited a conveniently short and movable distance upstream. This pillage left very little of the monuments of that king *in situ* at the

52. The temple of Amun at Tanis

53. Temple wall at Tanis, built from the reused blocks of earlier kings.

capital city he founded. The ancient history of reuse and rebuilding and the present state of the sacred structures at Tanis (figure 53) makes it difficult to reconstruct them in any detail. However, it is clear that, in one sense at least, the temple area at Tanis was even more important to kings of the Twenty-first and Twenty-second Dynasties than Karnak had been to monarchs of the New Kingdom. This was because it contained within its enclosure wall their royal tombs, a practice followed at other major quasi-royal centres of the Third Intermediate and Late Period in the Delta, most notably Sais, capital of a reunified Egypt in the Twenty-sixth Dynasty. Little is now immediately visible at this site, apart from traces of an enclosure wall which once surrounded a temple area of 455,600 square metres, making it one of the largest in Egypt from any period, but the description by the Greek historian Herodotus of the temple enclosure at Sais, which contained the burials of the kings of the Twenty-sixth Dynasty, suggests that in its day it was equal in magnificence to any temple in the land, including Karnak.

Apart from Tanis, the most significant surviving fragments of once impressive temples from this period in the Delta include a massive naos shrine in the temple enclosure of the ram god Banebdjed at Mendes, which was the home, and possibly the capital, of kings of the Twenty-ninth Dynasty, and a temple of Osorkon II and Osorkon III at Bubastis, the home of kings of the Twenty-second Dynasty. But, because of the amount of destruction, it is difficult to assess how innovative the major temple-building works of this period were. Tantalising glimpses like the Mendes naos, which was perhaps one of four in the sanctuary area of that temple (figure 54), suggest that the traditional standard-plan format was not regarded as sacrosanct in the face of innovation and the

54. The great naos shrine erected by Amasis at Mendes.

needs of particular local cults. In the south of Egypt most work consisted of adding to and embellishing existing temple structures. Because for much of this period the god Amun himself was regarded as 'king' of the vast tract of territory in southern Egypt under Theban control, the priesthood of Amun effectively ruled this part of Egypt and, not surprisingly, minor additions were made to Karnak.

Although the poor survival of the evidence makes it difficult to trace the architectural development of temple forms in the Late Period, it is likely that in the Thirtieth Dynasty, particularly under Nectanebo I and Nectanebo II, the origins of the major features of the architectural style which is considered typical of Graeco-Roman temples in Egypt can be detected. Both kings built on a massive scale, often using large quantities of hard stones, particularly granite, which is especially remarkable since most of their work,

55. Ptolemy II offers a necklace to the god Osiris-Wennefer at the temple of Behbeit el-Hagar.

now destroyed, was in the Delta, far from the source of the stone. This is most obvious at Behbeit el-Hagar in the central Delta, where both Nectanebos, followed by Ptolemy II and Ptolemy III, endowed a temple for the goddess Isis, mostly of granite and covered with reliefs of exceptional quality (figure 55), which was effectively the northern counterpart to Philae as a centre for the Isis cult. Behbeit el-Hagar survives now, like many major Delta temples, as a jumble of massive masonry. Similar continuations from the Thirtieth Dynasty to the Ptolemaic Period can be seen in the Delta from inscribed blocks of once splendid temples at Samannud and at the temple of Philae in Upper Egypt.

Temples of the Graeco-Roman Period

Building temples to Egyptian deities in Egyptian style was one of the most obvious ways in which Greek kings of the Ptolemaic Dynasty (332 to 30 BC) and Roman emperors (30 BC to AD 394) sought to legitimise their rule. In so doing they presented themselves as Pharaohs in a context in which the universal values of kingship and the monarch's relationship to the cosmic order were made manifest. It is ironic that the best-surviving temples, which epitomise the Egyptian architectural style as we now understand it, were built by non-Egyptian rulers to celebrate a belief system which was becoming ever more inward-looking and understood by a diminishing priestly elite. The 'hidden' and exclusive nature of these temples was emphasised by their carefully designed decorative schemes which presented obscure mythological dramas connecting the temple to the primeval universe, and increasingly obscure hieroglyphic systems of peculiar signs, designed by the priesthood of individual temples.

Upper Egyptian temples of the Graeco-Roman period are much better preserved than those of the north, although they were originally no more magnificent, and constitute the best group of surviving temples in Egypt. In many ways they dominate modern ideas of what an Egyptian temple is like, particularly that at Edfu, the best-preserved Egyptian temple anywhere, which was founded in 237 BC by Ptolemy III. Like many other Graeco-Roman temples in Upper Egypt, Edfu was built on a massive scale and swept away earlier smaller structures so that only traces of them remain, such as a partially preserved pylon base of Ramesses III. Like all Graeco-Roman temples, Edfu is similar in many ways to its New Kingdom predecessors, yet subtly different. The major parts of Graeco-Roman temples are identified by their own vocabulary; the heart of the temple, the sanctuary and its surrounding chapels, was anciently called the 'Great Seat' but is referred to by Egyptologists as the *naos*, a term which is used here in a much wider sense than its origins in the simple open-fronted box shrine which housed the divine

56. The Hathor-headed columns in the pronaos of that goddess's temple at Dendera. (Photograph: S. Thomas.)

image. In front of, but attached to, the naos was the *pronaos*, usually in the form of a hall both wider and taller than the naos and densely packed with columns. The pronaos was a development of the hypostyle hall of the New Kingdom but was a more prominent part of Graeco-Roman temples (figure 56) than most New Kingdom hypostyle halls (the great hypostyle hall at Karnak being an exception to this rule). It is also typical of the Graeco-Roman temple style in its elaborate, almost rococo decoration, its floral column capitals, the screen wall between the columns closing off the front of the pronaos, and its broken-arch gateway. The pronaos also occurs as the typical addition to existing temples by kings of the Late and Graeco-Roman periods, often replacing the pylon as the front of the temple, as it does at Dendera. Edfu is more usual in that a substantial stone wall surrounds both the naos and the pronaos, forming a corridor at the sides and rear of the temple, and an

57. The courtyard and pronaos of the temple at Edfu. (Photograph: S. Thomas.)

58. The sanctuary of the temple at Edfu, containing the naos shrine of Nectanebo II. (Photograph: S. Thomas.)

open courtyard at the front (figure 57), which is closed by a pylon gateway. In the centre of the naos at Edfu (figure 58) is the sanctuary, containing a black syenite shrine, over 4 metres tall, which was dedicated by Nectanebo II and must therefore have been reused from an earlier version of the temple.

Other structures common to Graeco-Roman temples include the room known as the *wabet*, a small chamber close to the sanctuary which was fronted by an open-air court where the New Year was celebrated (figure 59), and the *mammisi* or 'birth-house', a separate building within the temple enclosure designed to celebrate the birth of the god of the main temple or, if the temple deity was female, as at Dendera

59. The *wabet* at Dendera. (Photograph: S. Thomas.)

60. The *mammisi* at Dendera. (Photograph: S. Thomas.)

(figure 60), the place where she gave birth to her divine child.

The architecture at other Ptolemaic temples is more innovative than at Edfu. At Kom Ombo the foundation of Ptolemy VI has a unique double axis and twin sanctuaries dedicated to two gods, Sobek and Horus the Elder, with their respective divine families. Perhaps the single most impressive religious complex of the Graeco-Roman period is at Philae (figure 61), where an entire island in the Nile, at Egypt's traditional southern border near Aswan, was given over to temple buildings for Isis, a goddess particularly revered at this time, not just in Egypt but increasingly in other parts of the Roman empire.

The pagan cults of ancient Egypt gradually died out between the third century BC and the fifth century AD. Although Alexander the Great might have cause to venerate the oracle of the god Amun in the Siwa Oasis (figure 62), which pronounced him a god, and his successor

61. The temple of Isis at Philae during its resiting to Agilkia Island.

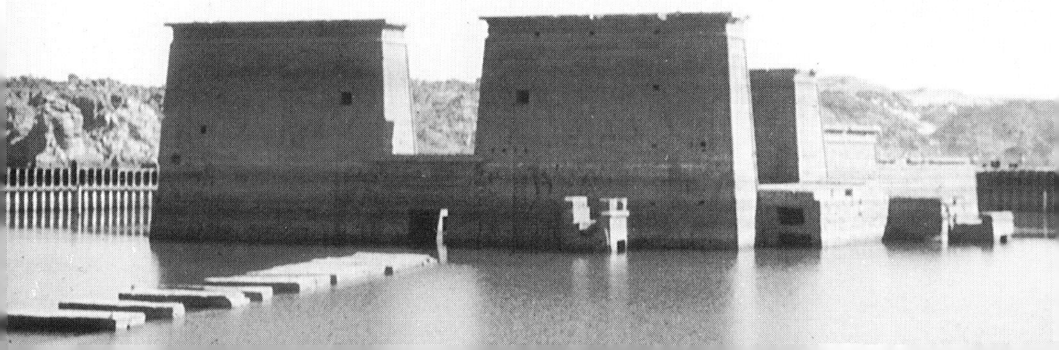

62. The 'Ammoneion', the temple of the oracle at the Siwa Oasis.

Ptolemaic kings patronised traditional cults and forms of temple building, the influence of Hellenistic philosophical thought among the educated elite began to erode the old religion. By the early fourth century AD the conversion of temples had begun, notably at Luxor Temple, which was now the centre of a Roman military camp and was adapted to celebrate

63. Romanisation of temples: the remodelling of Luxor Temple in the fourth century AD.

64. Christianisation of temples: a Christian cross replaces pagan symbols at Philae.

the emperor cult of the garrison. Even more serious was the arrival in Egypt of Christianity. The old temples and the rites practised within them were attacked by independent zealots like the monk Shenoute, whose favourite pastime seems to have been destroying temples in Middle Egypt. The sanctioned persecution of the pagans, when Christianity became the official religion of the eastern Roman Empire, was strengthened by a number of edicts, culminating in the mandate of Theodosius II and Valentinian III in AD 435. It was a fortunate abandoned temple which was allowed quickly to fill with drifting sand; others were demolished for their building stone, had their reliefs smashed, were converted into Christian churches (figure 64) or, at least in the case of Luxor Temple, provided the foundations for an Islamic mosque (figure 65).

65. Islamisation of temples: the mosque of Abu el-Haggag built over the first courtyard at Luxor Temple.

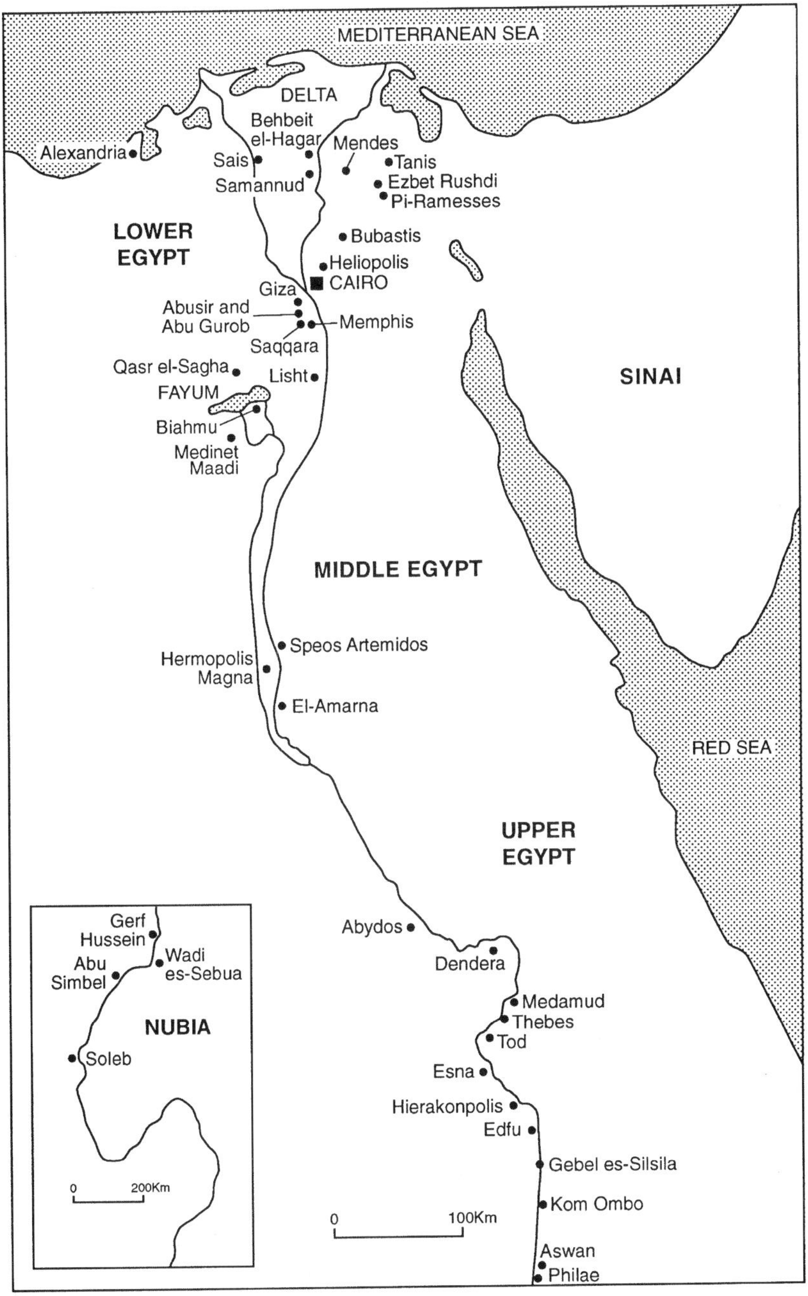

66. Map of Egypt, showing the locations of sites mentioned in the text.

8

Further reading

Arnold, D. *Die Tempel Aegyptens*. Artemis & Winkler, Zurich, 1992.

Badawy, A. *A History of Egyptian Architecture* (three volumes). Volume I, published by the author, Giza, 1954; volume II, University of California Press, Berkeley and Los Angeles, 1966; volume III, University of California Press, Berkeley and Los Angeles, 1968.

Baines, J., and Malek, J. *Atlas of Ancient Egypt*. Facts on File, Oxford, 1980.

Clarke, Somers, and Englebach, R. *Ancient Egyptian Construction and Architecture*. Dover Publications, New York, 1990.

David, A.R. *A Guide to Religious Ritual at Abydos*. Aris & Phillips, Warminster, 1981.

Edwards, I.E.S. *The Pyramids of Egypt*. Penguin, London, 1991.

Kemp, B.J. *Ancient Egypt; Anatomy of a Civilisation*. Routledge, London, 1989.

Reymond, E.A.E. *The Mythical Origin of the Egyptian Temple*. Manchester University Press, Manchester, 1969.

Sauneron, S. *The Priests of Ancient Egypt*. Evergreen Books, London, 1960.

Smith, E. Baldwin. *Egyptian Architecture as Cultural Expression*. Appleton-Century, New York, 1938.

Smith, W. Stevenson. *Art and Architecture of Ancient Egypt*. Penguin, London, 1981.

Spencer, P.A. *The Egyptian Temple: A Lexicographical Study*. KPI, London, 1984.

Index